CITIES AT WAR

TOKYO

★ ★ ★

David E. Newton

New York

Maxwell Macmillan Canada
Toronto

Maxwell Macmillan International
New York   Oxford   Singapore   Sydney

All photos courtesy of AP–Wide World Photos
Map on pages 8-9: Kathie Kelleher

New Discovery Books
Macmillan Publishing Company
866 Third Avenue
New York, NY 10022

Maxwell Macmillan Canada, Inc.
1200 Eglinton Avenue East
Suite 200
Don Mills, Ontario M3C 3N1

Macmillan Publishing Company is part of the Maxwell Communication
Group of Companies.

First Edition

Printed in the United States of America

10 9 8 7 6 5 4 3 2 1

Library of Congress Cataloging-in-Publication Data
Newton, David E.
    Tokyo / by David E. Newton. — 1st ed.
        p.   cm. —(Cities at War).
    Includes bibliographical references and index.
    Summary: Describes life in the Japanese city of Tokyo during World
War II.
    ISBN 0-02-768235-8
    1. Tokyo (Japan)—History—Juvenile literature. 2. Japan—
History—1926-1945—Juvenile literature. 3 World War, 1939-1945—
Japan—Tokyo—Juvenile literature. [1. Tokyo (Japan)—History.
2. Japan—History—1926-1945. 3. World War, 1939-1945—Japan—
Tokyo.] I. Title.   II. Series.
DS896.64.N48   1992
952'.135—dc20   92–2498

To Delores Horn,
my sister and, better yet, my friend

ACKNOWLEDGMENTS

This book was made possible through the kind and generous coop-
eration of a number of individuals who lived in Tokyo before, during, and after World War II. These individuals spent many hours
preparing for the interviews and talking with me. They not only
provided me with invaluable information and insights, but were gra-
cious hostesses to me. I cannot adequately express my appreciation
for their assistance.

Those who described their experiences to me were Yuriko Con-
nors, Kazuko Kiredel, Yukie Larson, Kinko Sone, Miyako Sueyoshi,
Reiko Thompson, Toshi Torgerson, and Toki Ushijima. Hisae
Cartier translated for her mother, Ms. Sone. Ms. Bridget Cooper
helped by translating for some prospective interviewees who spoke
little or no English.

In addition, Aki Mori spent many hours reviewing Japanese
books about the war and summarizing their contents for me.

A page from a Tokyo newspaper shows the damage done by the famous Doolittle bombing raid.

CONTENTS

★ ★ ★

The streets of prewar Tokyo shortly before the outbreak of war

1

A WORLD-CLASS POWER

The date for *Shichigosan* had arrived. In Japanese, *Shichigosan* means "seven-five-three." Each year, children who are 7, 5, and 3 years of age are honored at this festival. They wear their finest clothes on this special day.

In 1940, the most popular clothing among boys for Shichigosan was a military uniform. The boys dressed like admirals and generals. Most girls chose nursing uniforms. "Many wanted to be a Nightingale," Kazuko remembers. ("Nightingale" refers to Florence Nightingale, the founder of modern nursing.) Girls dressed as though they were ready to go to war at the side of their young admirals and generals.

Children in Tokyo, as well as adults, realized that their nation might soon be at war. The government had been preparing them for such a possibility for many years.

Preparing for war was nothing new for the people of Tokyo. For most of its early history, Tokyo was home to some of Japan's greatest warriors, and people had lived in the region of modern-day

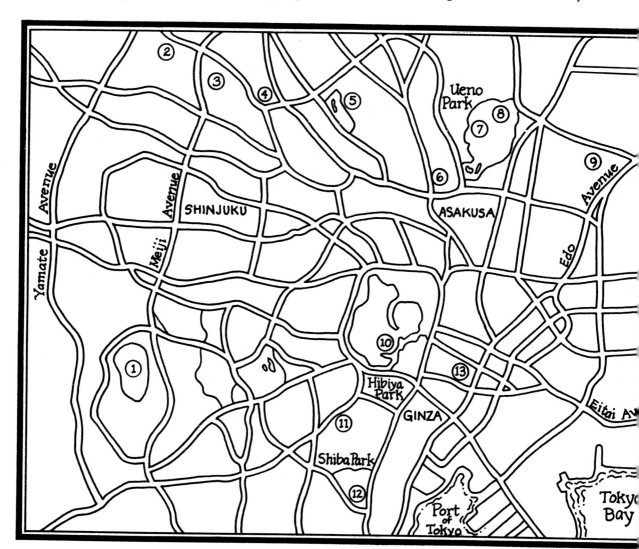

Tokyo as far back as 3000 B.C. This region—long known as Edo—
looked out over Tokyo Bay and a wide, flat area known as the Kanto Plains.

In about 1180, the military governor of Kanto built a castle
in Edo, but it soon fell into disrepair, and Edo became an unimpor-

① Meiji Shrine
② Rikkyo University
③ Kishibojin Temple
④ Gokokuji Temple
⑤ Koishikawa Botanical Garden
⑥ Tokyo University
⑦ Zoo
⑧ National Museum
⑨ Kannon Temple
⑩ Imperial Palace
⑪ United States Embassy
⑫ Zojoji Temple
⑬ Tokyo Station

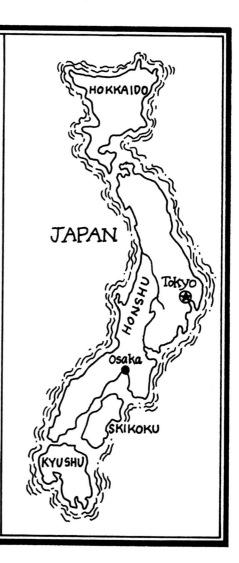

tant town for almost 300 years. In 1456, another warrior, Ota Dokan, rebuilt the castle at Edo. The year the castle was completed, 1457, is now regarded as the birth of the city of Tokyo. This time, a town, still called Edo, grew up around the castle. Houses, shrines, temples, roads, and ferry routes were all established.

Edo did not become a truly major city for more than a century. Then, in 1590, a warrior named Tokugawa Ieyasu chose Edo for his military headquarters. At the time, Edo consisted of no more than a few hundred simple, thatched-roof cottages.

But Ieyasu set out to build a great city on the site. He brought artists and craftsmen to Edo. He filled in the marshes around the city, built canals, and strengthened the castle. In 1603, Ieyasu became *shogun*, or military ruler, of all Japan. At the time, Kyoto was still the official capital of Japan and home of the emperor. But most political power now resided in Edo, where Ieyasu lived.

By the early 1800s, the population of Tokyo was well over one million. It was 15 times larger than that of New York City at the time and was probably the largest city in the world. During the rest of the century, however, the shoguns in Edo began to lose power. The city became much less important and by the 1850s its population dropped by about half.

The 1850s were a time of great change in Japan. Prior to that time, few foreigners had visited the country. The government feared that visitors from other nations would bring changes that would harm Japan. Therefore, it had banned all foreigners except a small group of Dutch traders.

In 1853, however, a fleet of American ships under the command of Commodore Matthew C. Perry arrived in the harbor of Nagasaki. Commodore Perry demanded that Japan open its ports

*The proud martial history of Japan is symbolized by these practitioners of
Kendho, the ancient art of Japanese fencing.*

to foreign trade. His fleet was so strong that the Japanese had no choice except to agree to his demands.

Change came to Edo once more in 1868. In that year, Emperor Meiji regained true power and decided to move his capital from Kyoto to Edo. Then he changed the city's name to Tokyo,

Victims of the tragic earthquake that rocked Tokyo in 1923

which means "eastern capital." Once again, new construction be-gan, and people flocked to the new capital.

The city was threatened by natural disasters, such as earth-quakes and fires. The most famous earthquake in Japanese history occurred on September 1, 1923. Most of central Tokyo was com-

Japanese infantrymen advance on Russian lines during the war of 1904.

pletely destroyed, and more than 100,000 people were killed. In addition, 1.5 million people were left homeless by the quake.

The Japanese people have learned to recover from natural disasters like fires and earthquakes. It took less than ten years, for example, for the people of Tokyo to completely rebuild their city after the 1923 quake. By that time, the city's population had reached 3.5 million. By the mid-1930s, the city looked much as it would at the beginning of World War II, less than a decade away.

Until the beginning of the 20th century, Japan was a small, powerless, unimportant nation, but that situation soon changed. In 1904, Japan went to war with and conquered its giant neighbor, Russia. The Japanese people were proud and thrilled. They had become a world-class military power.

The military strength of Japan on display

2

THE ROAD TO WAR

The 1920s were a decade of great change in Japan. Members of the military began to take a more active role in the government. Eventually they replaced civilians in all important government jobs. Military leaders were eager to expand Japan's influence in the world. They hoped to gain control over all of Asia.

The government began to prepare the people of Japan for a series of wars. The first would be fought against neighboring countries in East Asia. But the military knew that later wars would involve world powers such as Russia, Great Britain, and the United States.

In order to prepare people for the difficult times ahead, the government gradually introduced a massive propaganda program. Every possible method was used to get people accustomed to the idea of war and eager to do their part. Some mention of the glories of war appeared in every story, movie, book, newspaper, and radio program that was produced.

The government also began to make laws and regulations to govern the behavior of citizens. These rules affected every aspect of a person's life, from the most important to the least trivial. "Girls were not allowed to wear cosmetics or carry a fancy purse," Kinko says. "Children were told what kind of clothes they could wear and what color those clothes had to be, usually black or white. The government even set rules as to the hairstyles that I and my friends had to wear. Even the beautiful long sleeves of the traditional kimono had to be cut off."

These regulations were carried out by ordinary people. Certain adults in every neighborhood kept an eye out to make sure that children followed these rules. They reported the names of those who did not to the police, Kinko explains.

Regulations also prevented boys and girls from being together. Separate schools were set up for each sex. Boys and girls seen walking or talking together could be arrested by the police. This regulation applied even to brothers and sisters.

Government control also extended to people's ideas. The Peace Preservation Law of 1928 made it illegal for a person to even suggest changes in the national government. Anyone who broke the law could be put to death. Eventually the law was used by the government to imprison anyone who had "dangerous thoughts."

These laws had their effects on children, too. Reiko had ideas that were "different" when she was young. "But I could not talk with even my very best friends about these ideas," she says. "I was afraid that the government would hear about my ideas and, perhaps, take me away."

The first of the wars planned by the Japanese military began in 1931, when the Japanese army invaded Manchuria. It conquered

A symbol of Japanese tradition— a woman walks several steps behind her husband.

The Japanese flag, the Rising Sun, waves over conquered land in China.

the nation in a short war. Manchuria was added to the Japanese nation and given a new name: Manchukuo.

Six years later, Japan attacked an even larger neighbor, China. The Japanese were successful again, gaining control over a large part of northern China. By 1940, Japan had become a major power in East Asia.

Japanese children understood very little about these wars. Reiko recalls that she didn't know much about the outside world when she was young. "Perhaps great changes were taking place in Japan and the rest of the world," she says. "All I knew was the one small part of Tokyo in which I lived."

Some children learned about the battles in Manchuria and China. Many had fathers, uncles, and brothers who had fought there. When these men came home, they were treated as heroes. Yuriko was proud of her father. "He had been a soldier, and everyone admired and respected him."

Toki heard about China and Manchuria at the dinner table. Her father and uncles talked about the wars. "I never understood what was happening or why we were fighting," she says. "But I did know about the wars. Most of my friends didn't know any more than I did."

Japanese warriors were also honored in schools. The history books contained proud stories about another war, with Russia. Teachers pointed out how powerful the Japanese army had become. For the first time in history, other nations of the world respected and feared Japan.

To many children, the foreign wars seemed like happy and exciting times. People marched through the streets carrying flags and lanterns. Children often did not understand what the celebrations were about, but parades were always a lot of fun.

Young Japanese men learn the ways of war.

In addition, Japanese victories in Manchuria and China were celebrated in many schools. In Kazuko's school, "Students were all given a cookie that had a Japanese flag stuck into it. They marched around the school yard to celebrate the army's successes." Students

were happy not only because of the military victories, but also because they got to eat their cookies!

Still, the daily life of children in Tokyo and the rest of Japan
changed very little in the 1930s. The wars were very far away, across

The future of Japan: schoolboys participate in a military drill.

the seas. For many children, life was quite ordinary. Sometimes it was simple and difficult, while other times it was easier and more comfortable.

The life that Reiko lived during this time was probably typical of that of many young children in Tokyo. Her world centered around her family. "We lived in a small, five-room house in Tokyo," she says. "We cooked our food on a woodburning stove. We had to get our water from a well outside the door. We never had canned food or frozen food or dried food. Our mother cooked everything we ate."

Children who lived in Tokyo at the time have many fond memories of happy times: moon watching; strawberry picking; skiing; mountain climbing; going to the movies, theater, ballet; and playing children's games. A special highlight in Toki's memory was *tsuitachi*, the first day of the month. On that day, her father took all the family members and the servants to a restaurant for dinner.

One thing about life in Japan that was different was the emperor. For over 2,000 years, Japan had been ruled by an emperor or, sometimes, an empress. But the emperor was more than just a ruler. He was also thought to be a god. The Japanese believed that their first emperor, Jimmu Tenno (660-585 B.C.), was descended from the sun goddess Amaterasu.

Japanese children in the 1930s paid their respects to the emperor every day. Every school had a special place set aside for the emperor's picture. "It was the most important place in the school," Miyako says. "Every day students had to bow before the picture. If students showed disrespect for even the emperor's picture, it was a very serious offense. The school principal might have to kill himself, apologizing for the incident."

Japanese society in the 1930s was very different from that in the United States today. Young girls knew that they would someday marry and have a family. A girl's future in life was to take care of her husband and family. Few seriously thought of having an occupation other than being someone's wife. Most jobs in society were reserved for men.

Women did not even get to choose their husbands. Their families arranged their marriages for them. Neither the boy nor the girl had anything to say about the marriage and children would never have imagined otherwise.

Like girls, boys in Tokyo had few choices as to what their future would be like. Parents chose the schools to which they would go. They also chose the careers the boys would follow.

Obedience to parents has always been a tradition in Japan. Children in Tokyo in the 1930s were no different in this respect than Japanese children had always been. But the 1930s saw an increasing demand for obedience. In preparation for war, everyone—adults and children—had to obey the government's orders without question.

The Japanese government began planning for its next great war. Military leaders knew that their major enemy in that war would be the United States. By 1939, Great Britain, France, and other European nations were involved in World War II. These nations were unable to protect their colonies in Asia, such as Burma, Malaya, Singapore, and the Dutch East Indies. The Japanese believed that this would be a good opportunity for them to attack these defenseless colonies.

Only the United States seemed capable of stopping the Japanese. The United States had expressed its concerns about Japanese activities in China and other parts of Asia. The American government warned the Japanese to withdraw from China and stop

Japanese troops enter China.

Japanese prisoners of war are marched to a holding center.

spreading war in other parts of the Far East.

But the Japanese military refused to give heed to the American demands. This was partly because they would have been embarrassed about giving up lands they had already conquered. But they also doubted that the Americans could stop their military progress.

The Japanese believed that nothing could stop them from adding new lands to their growing empire.

When Japan ignored the warnings, the United States began cutting off the sale of vital materials to the Japanese. Tensions between the two great powers that faced each other across the Pacific

The results of the Japanese invasion of China.

Ocean grew stronger and stronger. In preparation for war, the Japanese government began a propaganda campaign against the United States.

The government told the Japanese people that Americans were monstrous, horrible people. They stirred up hatred and fear of Americans in every way that they could. Kinko recalls one incident in Tokyo in the late 1930s: "A group of army wives had placed an American flag on the sidewalk in downtown Tokyo. They asked shoppers to walk on the flag. They wanted people to show their hatred for Americans." But Kinko and her friends refused to walk on the flag. "Perhaps Americans were our enemies," she says. "But a flag—any flag—should be honored." So she and her friends just passed by.

Miyako learned in school that Americans and the English were *kichiku*, or "ogre animals," not really quite human. Later in the war, Miyako often wrote from an evacuation camp to her parents in Tokyo. She always made some mention of the kichiku in her letters. She knew her teachers read all her letters. "We could not write about our homesickness, but we could write about kichiku," she says.

Much of the information that Japanese children learned about the United States was incorrect. To Yukie, the United States must have seemed a tiny, weak nation, smaller and less powerful than Japan: "We were sure that the Japanese could win a war against the United States very quickly and easily." And that was just what the Japanese government wanted its people to believe.

The year 1940 was one of decision for the Japanese government. World War II had begun in Europe the year before, and most European nations were deeply involved in the fighting. The Japanese government decided that it was nearly time for Japan to join the war as well.

Japanese leaders made this decision for several reasons. Japan was a small nation, with a land area less than that of the state of Montana. But it had a large population—more than 70 million people. (The population of Montana at the time was only a half million.) Tokyo alone had a population of 7.4 million. There were more than ten times as many Japanese per square mile as there were Americans in the entire United States.

Also, Japan had few of the natural resources its industries needed. It had to import oil, steel, scrap iron, and other raw materials. It could not support a growing population and a growing industry with its own resources alone.

The purpose of fighting a war, they said, was to protect the Japanese economy. The government wanted to be sure that it would have a constant supply of the materials its factories needed. By conquering the countries that supplied these materials, Japan's economy would be strengthened. It also hoped to gain new lands to which Japanese people could move. It looked to Southeast Asia for these new territories.

Few children in Tokyo knew much about all of this. Toki was told that the war was "the only way we could survive. The country's economy was under great pressure." Children were taught that the country had no choice but to fight.

The Japanese government began looking for allies in other parts of the world. By 1940, Japan was very impressed with the sweeping success of the Germans in Europe. The government decided to form an alliance with the Germans and Italians. The Tripartite Pact was signed by the three nations in September of 1940. The Japanese thought they were joining forces with nations that would eventually conquer all of Europe. They hoped an alliance

Japanese troops prepare to invade Saigon.

Victorious Japanese soldiers take time out to celebrate.

with Germany and Italy would frighten the United States and Great Britain. The plan was for Germany and Italy to rule the Western world and Japan to rule Asia.

By this time, many Japanese had begun to think that war was a wonderful, glorious adventure. Victories in Manchuria and China had come easily. Japanese men, women, boys, and girls had been taught that the Japanese desire to win was stronger than that of non-Japanese. The United States and other nations might have more soldiers and better weapons, but that made no difference. Americans lived a soft, easy life. They had no desire to fight. *Yamato damashi,* the Japanese fighting spirit, would win out in the end.

Not all Japanese agreed. Some thought that going to war was a mistake. But it was difficult for these people to speak out. The government did not allow disagreement. One of Miyako's neighbors, a professor of economics, argued against the war. The police watched him. Another neighbor, troubled by his fear of the war, became mentally disturbed.

The major obstacle to Japan's conquest of Asia was the United States. Great Britain, France, and other Allied nations were busy trying to defend their homelands in Europe. They did not have the resources to fight a major battle in the Pacific Ocean as well. The United States seemed to be the only real threat to Japanese dominance in the Pacific Ocean. So, after long debate, the Japanese military government decided to launch a surprise attack on the United States.

American ships ablaze during the Japanese attack on Pearl Harbor.

3

WAR BREAKS OUT

The first Japanese attack came at dawn on December 7, 1941. It was aimed at Pearl Harbor in Hawaii, the major American military base in the Pacific. For the Japanese, the attack was a huge success. More than 3,000 American service personnel were killed or wounded. Nineteen ships and about 150 aircraft were also destroyed. In the raid, fewer than 30 Japanese airplanes were shot down and only about 60 men killed. World War II had begun for Japan and the United States, which until the Japanese raid had not officially joined the war.

The Japanese followed up on their success quickly. In the next six months, they overran the Philippines, Malaya, Singapore, Burma (now called the Union of Myanmar), the East Indies (now

Japanese soldiers ride into Hong Kong, one of the many countries captured during the war.

called Indonesia), Siam (now called Thailand), Hong Kong, and a number of Pacific islands. During the same period, their navy became masters of the Pacific Ocean.

The citizens of Tokyo, like those throughout Japan, reacted

with joy and excitement. It seemed only a matter of months before
the United States, like China, Manchuria, and most of Southeast
Asia, would surrender.

Young men in Tokyo were eager to show their patriotism.

Some wore shirts made of Japanese flags. Many tried to enlist in the army or navy as soon as possible. Most of Miyako's brothers' friends wanted to enlist in the naval academy. They wanted to become officers or naval fliers.

But Miyako's father would not let her oldest brother sign up for military service. A very important Japanese tradition was involved. Families want their names to be passed on from eldest son to eldest son "forever." Miyako's father did not want his oldest son to be killed. He insisted that his son enroll in engineering school. Engineering students were deferred from the military draft because the government needed some of its young men to become engineers.

Miyako's brother did not want to study engineering. He wanted to become a writer or a doctor. However, he understood the importance of tradition. He felt that he had no choice. He agreed to study engineering.

Miyako's second brother was not old enough to join the military. Still, all he thought about was the war. "He was always drawing pictures of airplanes and generals," Miyako recalls. He also memorized and recited the names of famous Japanese generals and admirals. Even today, 50 years later, Miyako can still remember hearing her brother say that list of names: Konoe, Shimada, Yamashita, Koiso, Anami, and so on.

At first, the war had little direct effect on the people of Tokyo. The fighting was taking place thousands of miles away. People knew only what they heard on the radio or read in the newspaper, and that news was all good. The Japanese army and navy were winning battle after battle.

The one exception occurred on April 18, 1942. On that date, Lieutenant Colonel Jimmy Doolittle led a U.S. bombing raid

A scene from the Battle of the Phillippines, one of many sea battles in the Pacific.

A plane takes off from a ship as part of the Doolittle raid on Tokyo.

on Tokyo. The raid involved only 16 U.S. bombers, and not much damage was done. Although the citizens of Tokyo were frightened by the bombing, there were no more U.S. air raids for more than two years. After the bombing, people in Tokyo began to feel safe again.

Gradually the war became more important in everyone's lives. Military training was introduced for boys in all the Tokyo schools. Each week, soldiers would come to Kinko's brother's school. "They taught the boys how to use guns," she says. "They had no real guns; but they used wooden rifles."

Kinko had already graduated from high school. She planned to work as a designer, but instead she was sent to a factory where bullets were made. Her life there was a good one. Since her job was important to the war effort, she was treated like a member of the military.

"I was not allowed to leave Tokyo," she recalls. "But I always had enough food and good clothing." Later in the war, her parents' home was burned down in an air raid, so she was allowed to move into a dormitory at the bullet factory.

Before long, many school activities centered around the military. Boys built model tanks that they drove around the school yard. They fought imaginary battles with wooden guns, while girls played along, helping out as nurses. School plays re-created war scenes. They showed Japanese soldiers winning great battles.

For one popular game, schoolboys dug a large hole in the school yard and made model airplane wings to fit on their arms. Then they ran around and around the hole with their arms outstretched. They looked into the hole to see what it would feel like to be a pilot looking down on a target.[1]

Schools began to place more emphasis on physical training,

Horses were an important part of the Japanese war effort. These sturdy ponies carried riders into battle in Manchuria.

too. Normally, students had to pass an examination to enter high school. The examination covered the Japanese language, science, math, and other topics. During the war, physical training was included in the entrance examination. Tokyo schools made students run while carrying a sack of rice. "My second brother was not strong," Miyako says, "so my mother took him to a special athletic class every Sunday to make him stronger." He needed to pass the athletic part of the examination in order to get into high school.

Before long, the people of Tokyo began to realize that war was not so wonderful. Gradually life became more difficult. Food became scarce. Good cloth was difficult to find. Even the quality of writing paper was poor. The war Japan thought it would win in a few months dragged on for more than a year, then two years, and more.

Children did not always understand what was happening. One of Miyako's next-door neighbors was a military officer, who often rode his horse to his home. "The horse always had good things to eat," she says. "I asked my father why our family could not eat as well as the horse. My father was very embarrassed. I wished that my father could be a military officer, too." What Miyako did not understand, of course, was that the horse was part of the war effort. To the Japanese government, Miyako and her family were not as important a part of the effort as the horse was.

Soon conditions grew much worse. The main problem was food. People were never able to get enough to eat. They were always hungry. Supplies for cooking and heating were in short supply also, with coal, oil, and gas difficult to find. They were all being used in the war effort.

Shortages led to rationing. Each family received tickets to use in buying food, clothes, and other items—when they were available.

A Japanese bomb sets a U.S. ship ablaze.

As early as December 1940, the government had set a limit of two-thirds of a pound (330 grams) of rice for each person per day.[2] But by 1941, even with rationing, there were no longer any rice or vegetables or fish, the important items in the Japanese diet. "We would all line up for just a bowl of soup," Miyako says. "Sometimes there was a little rice or noodles in the soup."

Waiting in long lines became a part of everyone's daily life. There were lines to buy food, lines to buy clothing, lines to buy fuel, lines for almost everything. Miyako's experience was typical. It was not unusual to stand in line at a bakery shop for a long time. "Eventually we were able to buy one small cake per person," she says, "which the whole family shared."

Kinko also remembers the food lines. "Sometimes I would wait in line for more than an hour," she says. "But then I found out I was in the wrong line, for clothes or even for a wedding. So I didn't have any food that day."

Everyday life in Tokyo had become very hard. Still, everyone wanted to support their nation in the war. "Our teacher told us," Reiko remembers, "that we should make every sacrifice for the good of the war. It's funny," she adds, "but I did not feel miserable. I always thought one must do and not complain."

★ ★ ★

The U.S. aircraft carrier Yorktown *endures Japanese attacks during the Battle of Midway.*

4

THE TIDE TURNS

In the summer of 1942, about six months after the attack on Pearl Harbor, U.S. naval forces won a great victory over the Japanese in the Battle of Midway Island. This was the real turning point of the war. Japan experienced its first great defeat, and its control of the Pacific Ocean was broken.

The government said nothing about the battle to its people. Instead, it continued to tell about great victories on every front. "As far as we knew," Yukie says, "Japan was still winning the war."

Changes on the front lines of the war did not make a great deal of difference at home in Tokyo. Whether Japan was winning or losing, conditions kept getting worse and worse. Food and other supplies had to go to the military. Shortages for civilians continued to be an everyday fact of life. Unless a family had relatives in the countryside, it usually had no way of getting food.

The children of Tokyo were still doing all they could to help the war effort. In 1944, the government required all high-school students to go to work in military factories. "We had to help make airplanes," Toshi recalls. "But no one complained. We were all happy to do that."

Reiko didn't talk with other people about the war. "But I was very sure that they would do whatever they had to. I think they went to war to win." For her own part, she was only sorry that she could not be a soldier: "I envied the people who could go and fight the enemy without any hesitation."

Schools had to find ways to solve the food problem for their students. In some cases, children were taught which weeds could be eaten and were sent into the fields to find them. The weeds were collected, left out to dry, and then were ground up to make flour. Weed flour was often the only food children had to eat.

Children also ate other unusual kinds of food, including grasshoppers, leaves, and raw beans. The beans came from inside their *otedamas*. An otedama is a child's toy, like a small ball, and consists of a cloth bag with raw beans inside. Many children got so hungry that they tore open their otedamas and ate the beans in them.[1] Another common food was *ama*, a plant from which linen thread is made. Normally no one would use ama as a food. But sometimes nothing else was available.

Miyako's brother searched for food. He often went into nearby stores looking for anything to eat. "The only thing he could find," she says, "was corn seeds."

There were other problems besides hunger— for example, a lack of medicines. People began to die of diseases that normally could have been cured quite easily. One of Miyako's brothers became ill with typhoid. He got the disease from eating corn seeds.

An American bomber cruises the skies over Japanese targets.

An area of Tokyo destroyed by a U.S. bomb raid.

Since no medicine could be found, he died.

Then, when Miyako's father tried to buy a casket, none was available. "There was no material to make one from," she says. Eventually her father found a suitable piece of wood and had a casket-maker make the coffin for her brother.

A new philosophy had begun to appear in Tokyo. As Reiko says, it was "more important to stay alive than anything else."

A second major turning point in the war occurred in July 1944, when the island of Saipan, in the Marianas, fell to U.S. troops. The loss of Saipan was a serious blow to the Japanese. For the first time in the war, U.S. airplanes, flying from Saipan, could reach Tokyo and the rest of Japan. Constant, massive bombing of the Japanese homeland began.

By the summer of 1944, the people of Tokyo had become very familiar with B-29s, the American aircraft that flew over the city nearly every day. Some days they dropped no bombs; they were simply taking pictures of the area. Many times, however, they covered Tokyo with a carpet of bombs.

"We got into the habit of putting our clothes away in a neat pile," Reiko says. "That way, when the B-29s came, I could get dressed very quickly and go to the bomb shelter."

One decision made by the Japanese government after Saipan was to remove all young schoolchildren from Tokyo. Two reasons were given for this decision. First, parents in Tokyo would be entirely free to spend their time working on military projects. Second, evacuation of all children would save the next generation of Japanese from death.

By August 1944, nearly every child in grades three through six had been moved out of Tokyo. Some children left with their own families. In these cases, the families normally had relatives living outside the city. Moves like this were very expensive, however. Only wealthy families could evacuate together. In most cases, the children went to stay with strangers in camps.

More than 80% of the children left Tokyo in groups. Usually a whole class or a whole school would be evacuated together. Teachers, principals, nurses, and children traveled together. The day Miyako's class left Tokyo, "the children gathered in the school yard to say good-bye to their parents. We all carried our backpacks and water bottles. None of the parents cried. They couldn't cry. We children smiled and sang songs."

Every school or district drew the name of its new location by lottery. Some went only as far as the suburbs of Tokyo. Later their new homes would give them a good view of the terrible nightmare that was to follow.

Other children went farther away, to rural areas, where they spent half a day in school and half a day working. Some helped with crops; others cared for cattle. Many children helped carry charcoal down from the mountains. Charcoal had become a vital fuel for use in military plants.

Children assigned to industrial areas also had work to do. They carried materials in factories, collected mulberries to feed silkworms, and helped with silk weaving.

Most evacuated students remained outside Tokyo until near the end of the war, although some sixth graders went home within a year. One sixth-grade class, which had been sent to Toyama in northern Japan, had a sad fate. The children wanted to graduate in Tokyo, at their own school. So officials allowed them to go back, but only for graduation. On March 15, 1945, while they were in Tokyo, one of the largest air raids of the war occurred. During the raid, all of the students were killed.[2]

A bomb blasts a chemical plant on the outskirts of Tokyo.

United States marines confront Japanese soldiers on Saipan.

*Most of the
children in Tokyo
were evacuated
to protect them
from the bombs
like the ones that
destroyed this
area of the city.*

Evacuated children were spared the horrors of bombing in Tokyo, but they were not spared many other terrible experiences, the most important again being hunger. As in Tokyo, the search for food was always first on everyone's mind. Even in farm areas, children were always hungry. There was just not enough food to go around. Principals and teachers spent all their time collecting food for the children.[3]

Children were also homesick, and many tried to escape and go back to Tokyo. Runaway children usually looked for railroad tracks. They knew they had come to the camp by train, so they decided to follow the tracks back home.

Often they walked the wrong way on the tracks, heading away from Tokyo instead of toward it. Townspeople often found groups of children walking along the tracks. They knew why they were there. They picked them up and returned them to the camps.[4]

"They didn't like to go back alone," Miyako says. "So they walked back in groups. They had to travel more than 20 miles to Tokyo. The children had to ask for money along the way. Even if they got home, their parents made them go back. The dangers in Tokyo were too great for them to stay."

Crowding was also a problem. Although camps were often set up in temples, Miyako's first evacuation camp was a school building. But when the military occupied the building, the children had to move into a temple. Students had no desks and very limited space of their own. They often had to sleep side by side, a dozen or more children in one small room.

Disease was yet another problem. Students had few opportunities to take baths. Infections were common. Once a disease got started in camp, it spread rapidly among the children. Eye infections were especially common.[5] Ironically, many children wanted to get

*Another casualty
of war: a
Japanese plane
shot down by
American fire.*

sick. Those who were ill were placed in private rooms and got better food. Some children even raised their own temperatures in order to appear sick.

Ticks and fleas were also widespread. Children got into the habit of checking one another for bugs. There was no other way to keep themselves free of pests.

Other problems developed in the camps, too. In many rooms, the largest, strongest child became a "boss." At mealtime, every child in the room was expected to give a spoonful of his or her food to the boss. Food and gifts sent by parents were taken away by the boss. Sometimes there was also physical abuse. The

weaker children could do nothing, since there was no place to escape. The situation was, in some ways, much like a gangster story.[6]

Conditions in Tokyo continued to get worse with each passing month. Some writers have described these conditions as "like hell."[7] Shortages of food, clothing, fuel, and other materials got worse and worse. "If you had relatives who were farmers," Yukie says, "maybe you could get food. But other people had a very difficult time."

One writer tells a story of children and an adult who fought over some spoiled food on the streets of Tokyo. The adult knocked the children down and took the food. "What a sad story," the writ-

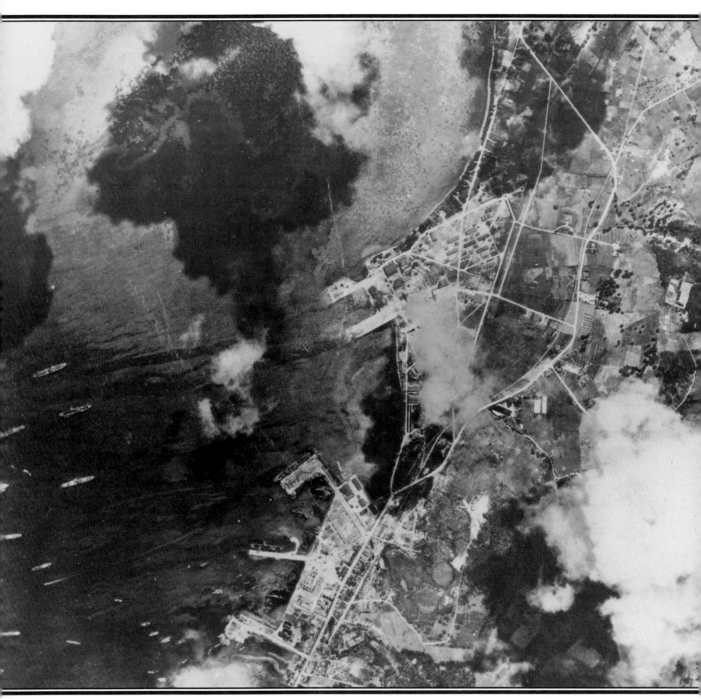

A Japanese military base seen from the view of an American bomber pilot

er concludes. "The children probably died of hunger, and the adult certainly died of food poisoning."[8]

Some people were more fortunate than others. Toki's father owned a dry-cleaning shop and also made his own soap. The soap was very valuable, even better than money. The family could exchange soap with farmers and fishermen for food and clothes.

Toki's family also planted a garden in their front yard. "We chopped down the trees that had been growing there," she explains. "Then we put in a vegetable garden. We also kept pigs and chickens in the yard." In addition, Toki's father went hunting and brought home small birds and animals to eat.

As the war developed, school became less and less important in Tokyo. After the loss of Saipan, a few high-school students went to school half a day and worked half a day. But most students left school and worked full-time in military plants.

Toki was a junior high-school student at the time. The school no longer held classes. "But we still had to pay tuition," she says. Instead of going to school, she spent her time sewing clothes for the military. Later there was no cloth to use for sewing, so she went to work in an army factory. There she did small chores for the other workers.

The one time Toki and her friends did study was during air raids. "When there was enough light," she remembers, "we could read and study in the underground shelters."

Hunger, loneliness, fear, and other ugly realities of war had now become commonplace in Tokyo and the rest of Japan. Yet, some of the worst horrors of the war were yet to come.

Like the bones of a skeleton, the shells of buildings are all that are left after a bomb raid.

5

BOMBING: THE ULTIMATE HORROR

By the end of 1944, another unpleasant reality of war had come to Tokyo: bombing. Except for the Doolittle raid of 1942, Japan had been spared the horrors of war on its own territory. But as the Japanese lost more and more Pacific islands to the United States, that situation changed. Adults and children in Tokyo became accustomed to seeing U.S. warplanes overhead nearly every day.

These warplanes brought with them the ultimate terror of war: death. "My friend and I left school one day and started for home," says Reiko. "Usually we walked home together. On this day, however, she went one way and I went another. After only two minutes, I heard an airplane overhead. Then I heard the sound of bullets hitting along the ground. I turned to look for my friend. She had been killed by the bullets."

Most people have stories of death to tell. Toki was in love with her brother's friend. "I was only 15 years old," she says. "So it was only 'puppy love.' But it was real love for me at the time." Her boyfriend was taken into the army. "He didn't come back," she remembers. Neither did her brother.

To protect against the bombings, shelters were built everywhere. In Tokyo, some shelters were built underground. Others were dug into the sides of hills. The shelters were large enough to hold many people. A whole school class could use just one.

These shelters worked quite well with ordinary bombs, but they did not work at all with the firebombs used later in the war. These firebombs not only caused explosions, but also spread flammable materials across an area. The firebombs turned the bomb shelters into fiery ovens. People were trapped inside and burned to death.

Individual homes also had bomb shelters, which were simply holes dug into the ground near the house. They were quite small, only a few feet deep, just large enough to hold all the members of the family. When the air-raid siren sounded, everyone in the family went to the bomb shelter.

"It was terrible," Reiko says. "It was so crowded we could hardly breathe. I preferred to stay in the house and take my chances with the bombs. Besides, I don't think the shelter really provided much protection."

Another protection against bombing were *bokuzukin*—cloth caps with cotton pads—that children wore to cover their heads during air raids. Children had to wear bokuzukin whenever they went out. "They really didn't provide much protection against bombs,"

The ruins of a once mighty city

Scattered buildings dot the demolished landscape along Tokyo's Sumida River.

Kazuko recalls.

The government prepared for bombing in another way: It tore down many homes in the city. Houses in Tokyo were built very close to one another. If one began to burn, the fire would quickly spread to others nearby. By tearing down houses, firebreaks could be made. Officials hoped that these firebreaks would prevent flames from spreading from house to house. They usually didn't.

High-school students did much of this work. One group of students sawed the posts on which a house was built. A second group of students tied ropes around the supporting posts. Then they pulled on the ropes. The house fell over quite easily.[1]

Many families suffered when their homes were torn down. If they had relatives, they could go live with them. But if they had no relatives or friends to take them in, they became homeless.

By 1945, Tokyo was suffering terribly from bombing by U.S. airplanes. A favorite technique of the bombers was to drop napalm sticks, pieces of wood covered with jellied gasoline. When the sticks hit a building, the building ignited immediately.

Bombing raids included anywhere from 3 to 500 planes. The fires that were created spread throughout the city, destroying homes and killing and injuring countless numbers of people. The worst air raid occurred on March 10, 1945. In that raid, more than 100,000 people were killed and an equal number were injured.

Residents of Tokyo in 1944 and 1945 can still describe the horrors of bombing. Even 50 years later, people can recall the dates of very large raids. For example, Yuriko talks about May 29, 1945, when 200 bombers flew over her home in nearby Yokohama and destroyed the city. Kinko remembers March 10 and April 13, 1945, when she saw "lights floating in the sky." The lights were flares that helped bombers find their targets.

American troops take back the island of Okinawa.

Kinko ran to her bomb shelter, but she could not stay there. "The smoke was so bad that we ran to nearby caves. We were blinded by the smoke. Our eyes burned so badly. We dipped our handkerchiefs in buckets of water on street corners that had been put there for that purpose. It was very scary. We could hear the B-29s right over our heads. But we couldn't see them because the smoke

was so thick. Everything around us was burning: houses, trees, bushes, buildings. The strange thing was that we saw so few people. Everyone had already left the city or had been killed in earlier air raids."

For some children, the strafing from airplane machine guns was more frightening than anything else. Yukie "could hear the rat-

The beginning of the end: Japanese troops surrender at Okinawa.

Their time ran out: cars in a Japanese parking lot become a grim reminder of the horrors of war.

tat-tat of the bullets making a path right next to us. It seemed as though the bullets were following us."

Everyone, including children, had to dig their own graves. No one knew when he or she might be killed in an air raid. The Americans had become very accurate with their bombing runs. Their carpet bombing would completely cover a narrow strip of land. "We thought we were going to die," Kinko remembers. "We had a pretty good feeling that this was going to be it."

Miyako was still at her evacuation camp during the worst bombing. Even from a distance of 20 miles, she could still see what was happening. "The sky looked like sunset," she says, "with fireworks going off. It was so sad not to know whether parents and grandparents, brothers and sisters, friends and neighbors were dying at that very moment."

For Reiko the bombing experience was "dreadful, horrible, awful. Sometimes when I close my eyes at night now, I can still see the redness." The ultimate horror of war—constant bombing—had finally become a part of everyday life in Tokyo and the rest of Japan.

Hiroshima after the atomic bomb

6

"WE WILL NOT FIGHT ANYMORE"

The newspapers carried a story about grass growing in Hiroshima. It was less than one year after the atomic bomb had fallen on the city. We all cried with joy. They had told us that it would be many years before anything would grow in Hiroshima. So there really was hope for the future.

— Toki Ushijima

In August 1945, the war came to an end. The final blow against Japan was the dropping of two atomic bombs on Hiroshima and Nagasaki. At least 250,000 people were killed or injured in these two bombings. The pair of air raids brought a sudden end to

American officers oversee the Japanese surrender on September 2, 1945.

the war. At midnight on August 14, 1945, the emperor decided that Japan had to surrender. Four years of war came to an end.

Some Japanese officials did not want to give up. They thought that Japan should fight to the very end, and they tried to convince the emperor to change his mind.

But the decision was made. The emperor made a tape recording to tell the nation that Japan had given up the fight. Kinko remembers that some officials tried to seize the tape recording. They thought that they might still be able to avoid surrender. More than one attempt was made to steal the tape as it was carried from the Imperial Palace across Tokyo to the broadcasting station.

These efforts failed, however, and the tape was played on August 15, 1945. The Japanese people heard that the war was over. Because he never spoke in public, it was the first time the Japanese people had ever heard their emperor's voice!

On September 2, 1945, representatives of the Japanese government, the United States, and other nations signed the official peace treaty. American troops began to move into Japan, taking over nearly every part of Japanese life. They were to remain in Japan for 6½ years. During that time, called the Occupation Period, the U.S. military controlled Japan.

The damage suffered in Tokyo was hard to measure. Nearly 100 square miles of the city had been totally destroyed. By some estimates, more than 800,000 buildings had been reduced to ashes. There was virtually nothing—homes, offices, factories, roads, bridges, canals—left of the downtown area. Most systems of transportation and communication had also been destroyed.

By the time the war ended, hundreds of thousands of citizens had fled from Tokyo to the countryside. Countless more had been killed. The city's population was 3.5 million in 1945, less than one-

Cleaning up after the destruction of Nagasaki

The T-shaped bridge in the center of Hiroshima was the landmark used in the dropping of the atomic bomb.

half what it was in 1940.

Most Japanese people were thrilled that the war had ended, including Toki, who was 16 at the time:

I went out into a small park and lay down in the grass. I looked up at the sky. It was so blue and so beautiful. I just cried and cried. At first I didn't know why I cried so much. But then I realized why. We lost so much. We had lost everything. Now I could escape the bad memories. Now I was alive. I could do something with my future. I didn't have to die.

The bomb dropped on Nagasaki destroyed almost everyting within a four-mile area.

Hiroshima begins to rebuild after the war.

Toki later learned that people all over Japan had similar feelings. From the southern island of Kyushu to the northern island of Hokkaido, the sky seemed especially blue on that day. "There were no airplanes, no bombs, no smoke. For the first time in many, many months," she says, "we could light our lanterns at night."

The end of the war finally gave people a chance to "let go" and express their feelings. Many children saw their parents cry for the first time. Miyako saw her mother weep over the son who had died of typhoid only a few months before. She had stored up all that sadness during the war. "It was the first time I saw the sorrow of a mother for her lost son," Miyako recalls.

Not everyone was happy that the war was over. Boys were especially angry that Japan had lost the war. They were sure they were going to win. Until the very end, the Japanese government had told them that they *were* winning; they only needed to hold on a little longer.

"All I ever dreamed about," says Toki's husband, "was going to the military academy. I wanted to be a fighting man. But after the war, I realized I had been brainwashed."

Returning soldiers had problems adjusting to civilian life. Many went back to high school. They had to start getting ready for college. But now they lived in a country controlled by their enemy, the U.S. military. They could not understand how the world's greatest nation (or so they believed) could come to this point.

Kamikaze pilots suffered the worst. These men had trained to die in battle. They were expected to crash their airplanes into American ships, killing themselves and destroying the ships. They had spent months and years waiting to die for their country. When the war ended, many were still waiting. It was very difficult for them to go back to a normal life in Tokyo. Many kamikaze pilots became drug addicts. They could never simply go home again and forget all they had seen and learned in the war.

Many children were angry because they knew adults had lied to them about the war. Some adults told children that Japan did not lose the war. "We simply stopped fighting temporarily. . . until you grow up. Then you can continue the war for us," they said.

Children did not accept that statement. They now realized that adults had been lying to them about the war. As to a continuation of the war in the future, the children's answer was "No way!"[1]

The war had destroyed some important bonds between children and adults. "I had always respected my teachers," Miyako recalls. "They were next to God. But I lost respect for teachers. I realized how much they lied to us about the war, and how they had showed us the ugliness of human reality."

Toki agrees. "We had been brainwashed about the war," she says. "We had to believe what they [our teachers] told us. But still I didn't believe 100%. I had questions." She also realized that news on the radio and in the newspapers had been false.

This doubt was new among children. Traditionally, Japanese children had respected and accepted adults completely. But the war had raised new questions. No longer did children feel that they could totally believe what adults taught them.

The war was over, but the suffering was not. For many children, conditions were as bad in peacetime as they had been during the war. Food was still very scarce. Kazuko thinks that food shortages were even worse after the war than during the war.

Miyako saw peanuts on sale in Tokyo for five yen, about two cents. "I asked my mother to buy me some peanuts," she says. "My mother said she couldn't afford the five yen. After that, I never

American servicemen survey the damage done in Tokyo.

asked her for anything else."

Clothing was in short supply, too. Used-clothing markets were very popular in Tokyo. Miyako had to wear her older brother's hand-me-down clothes.

Housing was also a problem. Many homes in Tokyo had been destroyed in the bombing, and families often had to move in and live with each other. In Miyako's case, up to six families were living in her house in Tokyo after the war.

Many children in Tokyo were frightened of Americans. They had been taught that Americans were "devils," "not like us," "not really human." Miyako had been taught that "Americans have red faces," like the demons in Japanese legends.

Children hid when they knew that Americans were coming to Tokyo. Miyako overheard her father talking about giving poison to her mother and herself so that they could commit suicide. "He didn't explain exactly why they should have the poison," she says. "But he wanted us to have it 'just in case something happened' when the soldiers arrived."

The day American soldiers first walked through the gate at her factory, Kinko hid behind the window in her third-floor office. She was terrified because she had been told that Americans were "rapists, killers, animals." "I felt like lions or tigers or other wild animals were coming to visit," she says.

Before long, however, children learned that American soldiers were not demons, but human beings like themselves. Many soldiers were kind and helpful. They often gave children chocolate bars and other treats. Soon, Japanese children were following "GI Joes" all over the streets of Tokyo.

Americans also helped the people of Tokyo recover from the damage of war. They brought all kinds of food for people to eat.

Rebuilding Tokyo

Kinko "survived only because of the food American soldiers brought. They gave us corned beef, which we had never seen before. But we learned to cook with it. And it saved our lives."

Miyako had a similar experience. "They gave us flour," she says. "But we had never seen so much flour before. We had never baked bread before." Eventually, they learned by inventing their own simple, homemade bread-maker. Her school lunches were also provided by the U.S. military. She "had dried milk, dried eggs, and tomato juice. I never got used to that food." It was very different from what the Japanese were used to eating, but it kept them alive.

Americans assisted in other ways, too. Many Japanese adults and children were covered with lice and fleas. They were highly embarrassed, since the Japanese are normally very clean people. But it had been extremely difficult to take baths and stay clean during the

Under American leadership, Japan rebuilt its cities and its pride from the ashes of the war.

war. When American soldiers arrived in Tokyo, they brought with them DDT, a white powder used to kill insects. From time to time, soldiers would spray Japanese adults and children with DDT in order to kill their lice and fleas.

Kinko stood in a train station one day when soldiers with DDT came by. "The soldiers sprayed us with DDT, and we were all covered with the powder. The Japanese people turned out white," she says, laughing. The experience was not a pleasant one, but it protected people from diseases carried by the lice and fleas.

Perhaps the most important thing Americans brought to Japan was a new way of life. Under the surrender agreement, the U.S. military took charge of every aspect of Japanese life. They wrote and imposed a new constitution on the nation, and they demanded that the emperor say that he was not a god. They outlawed all military forces in Japan, and they created a new curriculum for Japanese schools.

When schools reopened in Tokyo, students found many changes. Large parts of their history books had been blacked out. "So many things in the book were lies," Toki says. "The U.S. military removed all those lies."

Every morning, school principals recited three things to their classes: "One: All power rests with the people. Two: All people have basic human rights. Three: We will not fight anymore."

Japanese children began to learn about democracy. That does not mean that a complete revolution began to occur. In many ways, the most basic parts of Japanese life did not change at all. The roles of men and women and the place of the family in society, for example, probably changed very little after the war ended.

Yet, the ideals of democracy slowly began to have some effects on at least some Japanese children. For at least a few girls, the introduction of new ideas was especially welcome. They were glad to have more freedom to do what they wanted. For example, cultural organizations were created in some schools after the war. Boys and girls got together once a week to talk. "We were able to share our opinions about things. That never happened before the war," Yukie points out.

Customs began to change, too. Some young men and women began to choose their own marriages. Arranged marriages were still common. But for a few people, choices were available for the first time. "The younger generation began to look at the world differently from the older generation," Kazuko says.

Probably the most common memory shared by those who lived in Tokyo during World War II is just how terrible every day was. Toki puts it this way: "We lost everything, especially lives. People had no food, clothing, houses. My best friend's house was destroyed by a bomb. I never knew what the next moment would bring. Death was always behind me. Looking back, it seems like a gray, bad dream." Toki thinks this experience made her decide to become a nurse. After seeing so much suffering, she wanted to devote her life to helping others.

Kinko remembers the lack of food. "Everyone was skinny," she recalls. "We never had enough to eat. How surprised we were to see so many fat people when the American military came to Tokyo."

Reiko wonders what American children have learned from the war. "Will Hiroshima and Nagasaki open people's eyes?" she wonders. "Sometimes you have to make a mistake to know the right thing. I learned that war is not the answer. Will other people see that there is no more war in the future?"

Peace posters and the remains of a demolished building remind young Japanese girls of the horrors their country faced during World War II.

SOURCE NOTES

The information used in writing this book was obtained from two sources. First were a series of interviews with individuals who lived in Tokyo before, during, and after the war. These individuals were of elementary to high-school age at the time the war began. Three interviews were conducted in English. One was conducted in Japanese. For the Japanese interview, I relied on a translator for the interviewee's stories. Here is a list of those interviews.

April 23, 1991	San Mateo, California: Miyako Sueyoshi.
June 20, 1991	Security, Colorado: Reiko Thompson, Yuriko Connors, Kazuko Kiredel, Yukie Larson, and Toshi Torgerson.
July 9, 1991	San Bruno, California: Kinko Sone, translated by Hisae Cartier.
July 24, 1991	San Francisco, California: Toki Ushijima.

Wherever possible, I have used the exact words of those who were interviewed. In some cases, I have edited statements for grammatical reasons or clarity. All quotations reflect the spirit of the interviewee's own remarks.

The second source used in preparing for this publication was a number of books, written in Japanese, describing the experiences of children in Tokyo and the rest of Japan during World War II. All information cited in this particular publication was taken from one of these books, *Evacuation of Schoolchildren* (no author), published by Mainichi Shimbunsha (Tokyo), September 15, 1977. My translator for this book was Aki Mori.

CHAPTER THREE
1. *Evacuation of Schoolchildren.* Tokyo: Mainichi Shimbunsha, 1977, translated by Aki Mori.
2. *Kodansha Encyclopedia of Japan.* 1983. Vol. 8, p. 278. Tokyo: Kodansha.

CHAPTER FOUR
1. *Evacuation of Schoolchildren.*
2. Ibid.
3. Ibid.
4. Ibid.
5. Ibid.
6. Ibid.
7. Ibid.
8. Ibid.

CHAPTER FIVE
1. *Evacuation of Schoolchildren.*

CHAPTER SIX
1. *Evacuation of Schoolchildren.*

FURTHER READING

✱ ✱ ✱

To the best of my knowledge, there are no books in English that deal specifically with the experiences of children in Tokyo during World War II. In fact, none of the histories of that period provide more than a brief mention of the special experiences of children at the time.

A number of books provide good descriptions of the general culture and history of Japan and Tokyo just before and during the war. Among the best of these are the following:

Fairchild, Johnson E., et al. *The World and its Peoples: Japan* (2 vols). New York: Greystone Press, 1964.

Kennedy, Malcolm D. *A Short History of Japan*. New York: Mentor Books, 1963.

Kodansha Encyclopedia of Japan. Tokyo: Kodansha, 1983. [See especially the entries under "Tokyo" and "World War II."]

Mariani, Fosco, and the editors of Time-Life Books. *Tokyo* (Great Cities of the World series). Amsterdam: Time-Life Books, 1976.

Morris, John. *Traveler from Tokyo*. New York: Sheridan House, 1944.

Nishida, Kazuo. *Storied Cities of Japan*. Tokyo: John Weatherhill, 1963.

Tiedemann, Arthur E. *An Introduction to Japanese Civilization*. New York: Columbia University Press, 1974.

INDEX

★ ★ ★